LANDMARKS IN MY COMMUNITY

THE MUSEUM

BY SADIE SILVA

Gareth Stevens
PUBLISHING

Please visit our website, www.garethstevens.com. For a free color catalog of all our high-quality books, call toll free 1-800-542-2595 or fax 1-877-542-2596.

Library of Congress Cataloging-in-Publication Data
Names: Silva, Sadie, author.
Title: The museum / Sadie Silva.
Description: Buffalo, NY : Gareth Stevens Publishing, 2025. | Series: Landmarks in my community | Includes index.
Identifiers: LCCN 2023034769 (print) | LCCN 2023034770 (ebook) | ISBN 9781538293164 (library binding) | ISBN 9781538293157 (paperback) | ISBN 9781538293171 (ebook)
Subjects: LCSH: Museums–Juvenile literature.
Classification: LCC AM5 .S5735 2025 (print) | LCC AM5 (ebook) | DDC 069–dc23/eng/20230814
LC record available at https://lccn.loc.gov/2023034769
LC ebook record available at https://lccn.loc.gov/2023034770

Published in 2025 by
Gareth Stevens Publishing
2544 Clinton Street
Buffalo, NY 14224

Designer: Andrea Davison-Bartolotta
Editor: Caitie McAneney

Photo credits: Cover, p. 1 christiancarollo/iStockphoto.com; series art (page numbers) art_of_sun/Shutterstock.com; series art (map background) Marian Salabai/Shutterstock.com; p. 5 legacy1995/Shutterstock.com; p. 7 BearFotos/Shutterstock.com; p. 9 posztos/Shutterstock.com; pp. 11, 17 Monkey Business Images/Shutterstock.com; pp. 13, 15 SeventyFour/Shutterstock.com; p. 19 Viacheslav Lopatin/Shutterstock.com; p. 21 Popova Valeriya/Shutterstock.com.

Printed in the United States of America

CPSIA compliance information: Batch #CS25GS: For further information contact Gareth Stevens, New York, New York at 1-800-542-2595.

CONTENTS

Boldface words appear in the glossary.

Time to Learn!

Imagine you love dinosaurs. Where can you learn about them? You can go to a museum to see dinosaur bones! Museums have **information** and objects to help you learn about many different things.

THE NATION BEHAVES WELL IF IT
TREATS THE NATURAL RESOURCES
AS ASSETS WHICH IT MUST TURN
OVER TO THE NEXT GENERATION
INCREASED AND NOT IMPAIRED
IN VALUE
CONSERVATION MEANS DEVELOPMENT
AS MUCH AS IT DOES PROTECTION
5

What Is a Museum?

A museum is a building where important objects are kept. Some objects are old, such as dinosaur bones or **historical** papers. Other objects are new, such as some pieces of art. Museum objects help us understand the world, past and present.

Different Kinds of Museums

You can visit different kinds of museums. History museums have historical objects and information. Some museums cover natural history, or things in nature. Others cover events in human history. Art museums have art from the past and present.

AMERICAN MUSEUM OF NATURAL HISTORY NEW YORK, NY

Science museums have different **exhibits** that deal with space, bugs, **engineering**, and more! Many science museums have hands-on **sections** for kids. Play museums have many hands-on exhibits. Kids can explore toys and games from the past and present.

Visiting the Museum

Anyone can visit a museum! Some are free and some cost money. Big cities often have big museums. Smaller towns may have a smaller museum about town history. You can walk around the exhibits that interest you.

Meet Museum Workers!

Many people work in a museum. Some workers clean the exhibits. Some answer questions that guests have. Museum curators decide what goes in each exhibit. They choose special objects that fit together to teach people about something.

Museums for All

Museums are important community places because anyone can visit. Anyone can learn something new from the exhibits! Schools often bring students to museums to learn about history and science. Some people want to learn more about their **culture**.

GREEKS ON THE BLACK SEA

Museums are important because they hold objects that you may never see anywhere else. Some have **artifacts** from thousands of years ago. Some have space rocks, paintings, or historical clothing. Seeing these objects firsthand makes learning fun for everyone!

ARTIFACTS, GREECE

Your Community Museum

Does your community have a museum? Ask your parents or teachers if you can visit your community museum. It might teach you about life in your community and the world outside of it. You can learn a lot from a museum!

GLOSSARY

artifact: Something made by humans in the past.

culture: The beliefs and ways of life of a group of people.

engineering: The use of science and math to build something.

exhibit: Things that are put together in a collection for people to look at.

historical: Having to do with the past.

information: Knowledge or facts that come from a source.

section: Any part of a whole.

FOR MORE INFORMATION

BOOKS

Amin, Anita Nahta. *Amazing Museums*. Minneapolis, MN: Jump! Inc., 2023.

Mabbitt, Will. *Lost in the Museum: A Seek-and-Find Adventure in The Met*. London, UK: DK Children, 2021.

WEBSITES

Fun Facts for Kids
americanhistory.si.edu/kids/fun-facts-kids
Learn about some of the objects you can find at the National Museum of American History.

Museum
kids.kiddle.co/Museum
Explore fun facts about different kinds of museums.

INDEX